HOW
ANGELS
GET THEIR
WINGS

BY BONNIE ALTENHEIN
Illustrations by Monica Sheehan

WINGS BOOKS • NEW YORK • AVENEL

This 1994 edition is published by Wings Books,
distributed by Random House Value Publishing, Inc.,
40 Engelhard Avenue, Avenel, New Jersey 07001,
by arrangement with the author.

Random House
New York • Toronto • London • Sydney • Auckland

Printed and bound in the United States of America

Library of Congress Cataloging-in-Publication Data

Altenhein, Bonnie.
   How angels get their wings / by Bonnie Altenhein ; illustrations by
Monica Sheehan.
      p.   cm.
   ISBN 0-517-10080-0
   1. Conduct of life.   2. Conduct of life—Humor.   I. Title.
BJ1581.2.A44   1994
170'.44—dc20   94-8334
                                                                  CIP

   8   7   6   5   4

DEDICATION

This book is dedicated with love to my mother, Pauline, who is up there somewhere playing *Jeopardy!* with June and the angels, and Jonathan, a special angel.

ACKNOWLEDGEMENTS

With appreciation to all the angels who have touched my life: Allen, Anita, Archie and Adele, Barbara, Beau, Ben and Marypat, Deborah, Edie, Frank, George, Gerri, Irene, Jackie, Jeff, Joanna, Judi, Julie, Kate, Kaitlyn and Jessica, Laurie, Louise, Marsha, Mitchell, Rohanna, Sil, and Suli.

Perhaps we are all really angels-in-training, learning as we go to laugh, to love and to grow. This little manual of "angelosophy" is a guidebook for all the earth angels trying to earn their wings. Maybe in the process, we can make this world a little bit better and brighter for ourselves and our fellow angels.

ngels are the guardians
of hope and wonder, the keepers
of magic and dreams.

1

Angels travel light
and simple.

It's easy to fly when you take yourself lightly.

Whenever you hear a bell ring, another angel has earned her wings.

5

Touch someone softly
with your wing.

6

Angels never postpone joy
to scrub the bathroom floor.

8

ngels leave space in their
relationships so there's lots of
room to play.

9

Remember that beauty
comes in petite, half-sizes
and everything in between.

10

Angels always carry a
spare set of wings in
their pocket.

12

Angels send a rainbow in with their tax return.

13

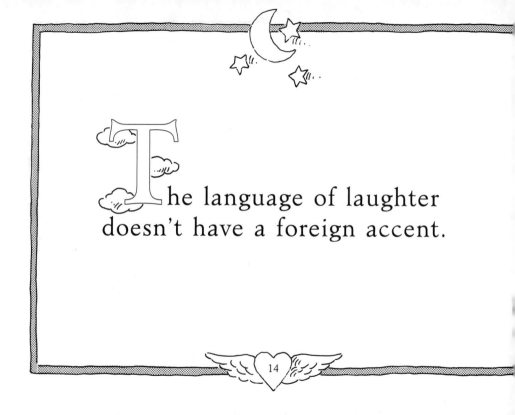

The language of laughter
doesn't have a foreign accent.

14

Whenever you need advice,
look in the mirror
and ask.

16

Remember your mother was probably right.

17

Be an angel on call
for a friend.

18

Listen to your inner heart
for the best advice.

20

Cherish your special
idiosyncracies.

21

ngels can always tune
out the commercials of life.

22

Love is the only four-letter word you need to know.

ngels measure life in
miracles, not errands
and chores.

Follow your heartlight.

26

Angels dare to be delightful.

28

Your higher power is never hard to reach.

Don't hide your light
under a lampshade.

30

If things go wrong, you don't
have to go with them.

32

Angels look out for the
rain forests.

33

It's very okay to cry
during sad movies.

34

For this moment, you are doing the best that you can.

36

An angel adopts grinning
as a second language.

37

ngels take a moonbath, a
snowbath or a bubble bath
everyday.

38

It's never too late to create a happy childhood.

40

If you're too full of yourself,
there is no room left for love.

41

ngels know all the
possibilities of their
impossible dream.

42

An angel's dictionary doesn't have "shoulda", "coulda", "oughta", or "can't".

44

The road to your personal
somewhere never follows a
crowd.

45

Each morning brings your
wake-up call from the universe.

Angels step lightly
into love rather than fall head
over heels.

Open your umbrella before
it rains on your parade.

49

The kindest mirror is the reflection of a dear friend.

50

If there is no happy ending for today, write a new chapter called tomorrow.

An angel can invent 100 ways to say, "I'm sorry".

53

Make a date with a daydream.

54

Refine the art
of making up.

56

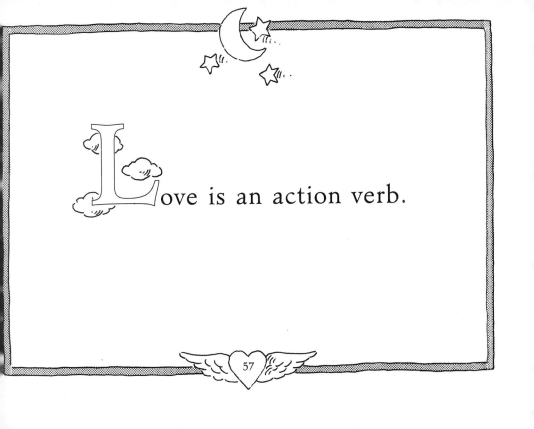

Love is an action verb.

ngels practice telling
jokes.

An angel's epitaph is never, "I wish I'd spent more time at the office".

Angels know it's silly
not to be silly.

Write a personal instruction manual for your own life.

ngels keep it simple.

64

ngels forgive, forget and
forge ahead.

65

Invite a friend for a joy ride
on your mood swing.

66

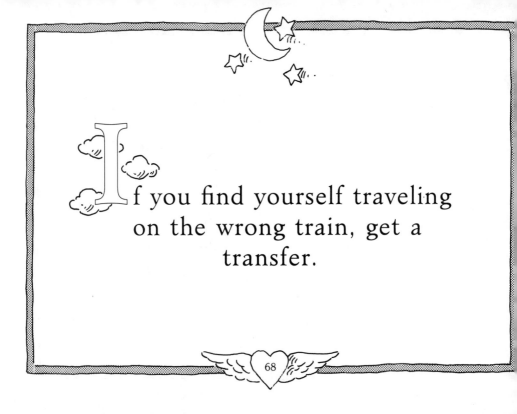

If you find yourself traveling on the wrong train, get a transfer.

68

Sunshine and a lover's
quarrel disappear with the
nightfall.

Dust out your anxiety
closet and sweep the fears away.

70

Angels keep a journal of
all their hopes and dreams.

72

Take the "r" out of your anger and replace it with an "l".

Angels talk to the animals.

74

ngels always follow
their passion.

76

Angels know that self-love
is never unrequited.

77

ngels love and respect
Mother Earth.

You are dealt a royal flush:
keep what fits in your hand,
discard what doesn't work.

Angels are not afraid to
say "I don't know".

81

You can't win the lottery
unless you buy a ticket.

Don't live in the future
now: that's where you'll be
spending the rest of your life.

ngels count all the colors
of a spectacular sunset.

85

Do something wonderful
for someone who will never
know it was you.

86

Life works better if you pretend every day is Friday afternoon.

88

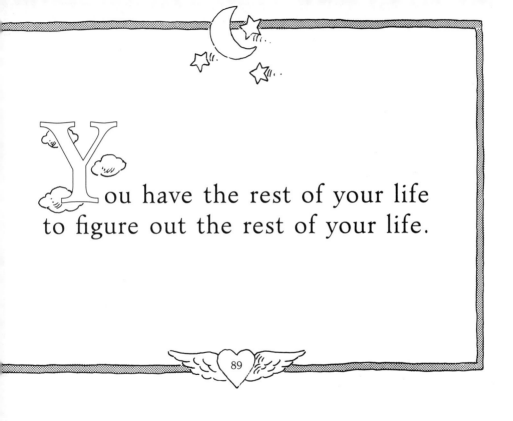

You have the rest of your life
to figure out the rest of your life.

Bonnie Altenhein was born and raised in New York City, and has been writing about everything from angels to zebras since she was old enough to hold a crayon. She was an editor of *Better Homes and Gardens* magazine, former secretary and "joke coordinator" for Joan Rivers, and creator of WATCH MY LIPS!—a unique, million-dollar company that developed a line of "greeting seed" cards that became an overnight industry phenomenon. She has been featured in *Business Week, Advertising Age,* and other publications.

Nominated several times for the "Louie" award—the highest honor for greeting card writers—Ms. Altenhein is a free-lance writer/designer and the author of a bestselling calendar, poster, and several greeting cards featuring angels. HOW ANGELS GET THEIR WINGS is her first book.

A lifetime student of "angel-osophy", Bonnie has a son named Jonathan and a guardian angel named "Frieda." Both are helping her finish a novel.